ENGINEERING MARVELS

HOOVER DAM

by Nikole Brooks Bethea

pogo

Ideas for Parents and Teachers

Pogo Books let children practice reading informational text while introducing them to nonfiction features such as headings, labels, sidebars, maps, and diagrams, as well as a table of contents, glossary, and index.

Carefully leveled text with a strong photo match offers early fluent readers the support they need to succeed.

Before Reading

- "Walk" through the book and point out the various nonfiction features. Ask the student what purpose each feature serves.
- Look at the glossary together. Read and discuss the words.

Read the Book

- Have the child read the book independently.
- Invite him or her to list questions that arise from reading.

After Reading

- Discuss the child's questions. Talk about how he or she might find answers to those questions.
- Prompt the child to think more. Ask: Have you ever seen a dam, either in person or in a photograph?

Pogo Books are published by Jump!
5357 Penn Avenue South
Minneapolis, MN 55419
www.jumplibrary.com

Library of Congress Cataloging-in-Publication Data

Names: Bethea, Nikole Brooks, author.
Title: Hoover Dam / by Nikole B. Bethea.
Description: Minneapolis, MN: Jump!, Inc., [2017]
Series: Engineering marvels | Includes bibliographical references and index.
Identifiers: LCCN 2017004843 (print)
LCCN 2017005325 (ebook)
ISBN 9781620317013 (hard cover: alk. paper)
ISBN 9781624965784 (e-book)
Subjects: LCSH: Hoover Dam (Ariz. and Nev.)–Juvenile literature.
Dams–Design and construction–Juvenile literature.
Water-supply–Southwest, New–Juvenile literature.
Water-power–Juvenile literature.
Classification: LCC TC557.5.H6 B48 2017 (print)
LCC TC557.5.H6 (ebook) | DDC 627.820979313–dc23
LC record available at https://lccn.loc.gov/2017004843

Editor: Kirsten Chang
Book Designer: Molly Ballanger
Photo Researcher: Molly Ballanger

Photo Credits: Susan E. Degginger/Alamy, cover; albertczyzewski/Shutterstock, 1; Eunika Sopotnicka/Shutterstock, 3; john michael evan potter/Shutterstock, 4; Claude Huot/Shutterstock, 5; Ed Endicott/Alamy, 6-7; Mike Richter/Thinkstock, 8-9; Bettmann/Getty, 10; George Rinhart/Getty, 11; University of Southern California/Getty, 12-13, 14-15; Lowe Llaguno/Shutterstock, 16-17; Maciej Bledowski/Shutterstock, 18; Bokic Bojan/Shutterstock, 19; Zainkapasi/Dreamstime, 20-21; Chad Kanera/Dreamstime, 23.

Printed in the United States of America at Corporate Graphics in North Mankato, Minnesota.

TABLE OF CONTENTS

CHAPTER 1

CONTROLLING THE RIVER

What can hold back a river and power a city? A **dam**!

Hoover Dam is one of the most impressive dams in the world. It is an engineering marvel. And it was built to fix a real-world problem.

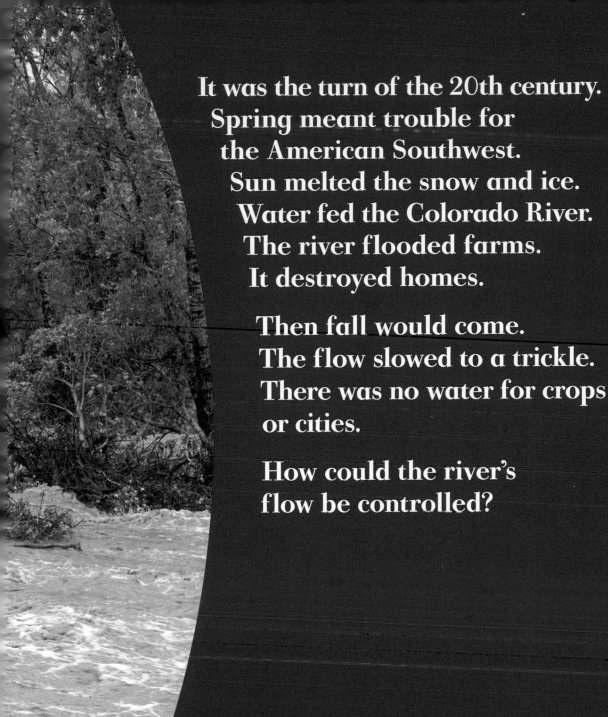

It was the turn of the 20th century.
Spring meant trouble for
the American Southwest.
Sun melted the snow and ice.
Water fed the Colorado River.
The river flooded farms.
It destroyed homes.

Then fall would come.
The flow slowed to a trickle.
There was no water for crops
or cities.

How could the river's
flow be controlled?

Engineer Arthur P. Davis had an idea. He wanted to build a big dam. A **reservoir** would form behind it. It would store floodwaters. The water could be sent to areas that needed it. The dam could also make electricity for people nearby.

DID YOU KNOW?

Hoover Dam's reservoir is called Lake Mead. The water it stores could flood Pennsylvania one foot (0.3 meters) deep!

Lake Mead
Reservoir

CHAPTER 2

BUILDING THE DAM

Work on the dam began in 1931. The first step was to dig tunnels through the **canyon** walls. The river would flow through them. This would clear the way for construction. Boom! Dynamite blasted the rock.

Workers drilled four tunnels. Rocks removed from the tunnels were dumped in the river. The water was blocked. It rushed through the tunnels. The job site was clear.

The next step was to clear rock from the canyon walls. Men climbed down the canyon on ropes. They drilled holes in the walls and inserted dynamite. This was a very dangerous job. Dozens of men died.

Once the walls were clear, the dam was built. It took huge amounts of **concrete**. It was built block by block. Cold water pipes ran through each block. This helped them cool.

When it was finished in 1936, it was the world's tallest dam. It rises 726 feet (221 m) from the canyon floor. That's about as tall as 126 men. It is 660 feet (201 m) thick at the base. That's about the length of two football fields!

spillway

The top of the dam is 45 feet (13.7 m) thick. **Spillways** are on both sides. If water rises high enough, it drains into the spillways. Each one could handle the flow from Niagara Falls.

TAKE A LOOK!

Hoover Dam is an arch dam. It is curved.
What other types of dams are there?

ARCH

EMBANKMENT

GRAVITY

BUTTRESS

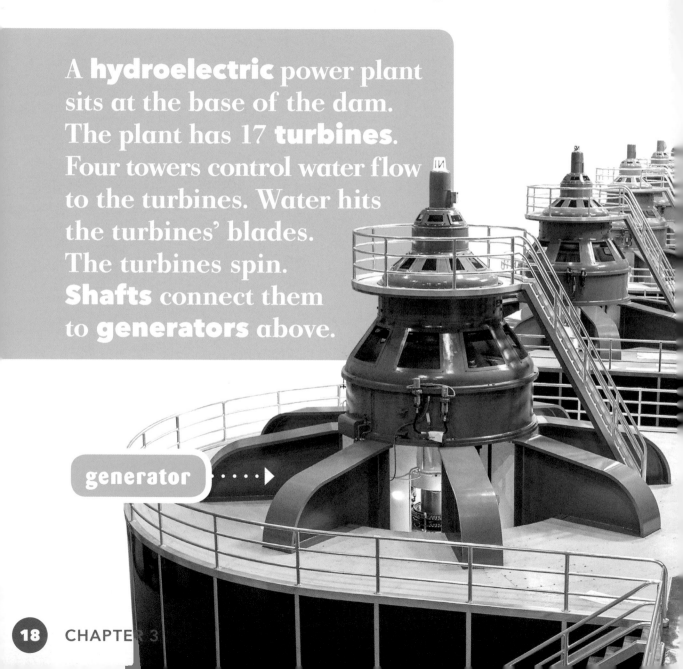

CHAPTER 3

MAKING POWER

A **hydroelectric** power plant sits at the base of the dam. The plant has 17 **turbines**. Four towers control water flow to the turbines. Water hits the turbines' blades. The turbines spin. **Shafts** connect them to **generators** above.

generator ····▶

Inside, magnets spin in copper coils. This makes electricity. The plant makes power for 1.3 million people in the Southwest.

Engineers have named Hoover Dam one of America's Seven Modern Civil Engineering Wonders. About a million people tour the dam each year. Maybe one day you will see this marvel for yourself!

ACTIVITIES & TOOLS

BUILD A DAM

Your task is to build a dam that will prevent water from leaking from one side of a container to the other.

What You Need:
- long, shallow plastic container
- popsicle sticks
- modeling clay
- rocks and gravel
- pitcher of water

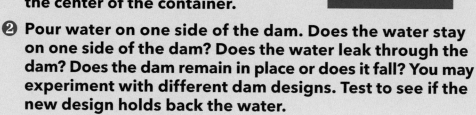

❶ Use the clay, popsicle sticks, rocks, and gravel to build a dam across the center of the container.

❷ Pour water on one side of the dam. Does the water stay on one side of the dam? Does the water leak through the dam? Does the dam remain in place or does it fall? You may experiment with different dam designs. Test to see if the new design holds back the water.

GLOSSARY

canyon: A deep valley with steep sides of rock.

concrete: Hard material that is made by mixing cement, rocks, and sand with water.

dam: A structure built across a waterway that blocks the flow of water.

engineer: A scientist who uses math and science to solve problems and create things that humans use.

generators: Machines that produce electricity.

hydroelectric: Relating to the generation of electricity from flowing or falling water.

reservoir: A man-made lake used to store water.

shafts: Bars or poles that transmit power or rotating motion.

spillways: Channels or passages of surplus water from a dam.

turbines: Devices that convert the energy of a moving fluid into rotary motion to spin a generator.

INDEX

TO LEARN MORE

Learning more is as easy as 1, 2, 3.

1) Go to www.factsurfer.com

2) Enter "HooverDam" into the search box.

3) Click the "Surf" button to see a list of websites.

With factsurfer, finding more information is just a click away.